# Tara Lipinski

## Additional Titles in the Sports Reports Series

# Tara Lipinski

## Star Figure Skater

Barry Wilner

**Enslow Publishers, Inc.**

| | |
|---|---|
| 40 Industrial Road | PO Box 38 |
| Box 398 | Aldershot |
| Berkeley Heights, NJ 07922 | Hants GU12 6BP |
| USA | UK |

http://www.enslow.com

## Acknowledgments

The writing of this book would not have been possible without the help and understanding of my wife, Helene, daughters, Nicole, Jamie, and Tricia, and son, Evan.

I would also like to acknowledge the contributions of:
Nancy Armour, Colleen Barry, Mike Burg, Richard Callaghan, Frank Carroll, Bob Dunlop, Todd Eldredge, Heather Linhart, Marie Millikan, Deb Nast, Lynn Plage, B.J. Reyes, Amy Rosewater, Gerri Walbert, Joseph White, and Sal Zanca.

**Library of Congress Cataloging-in-Publication Data**

Wilner, Barry.
Tara Lipinski: star figure skater / Barry Wilner.
      p.  cm. – (Sports reports)
Includes bibliographical references (p.  ) and index.
ISBN 0-7660-1505-X
1. Lipinski, Tara, 1982—Juvenile literature. 2. Skaters—United States—Biography—Juvenile literature. [1. Lipinski, Tara, 1982– . 2. Ice skaters. 3. Women—Biography.]
I. Title. II. Series.
GV850.L56 W56 2001

796.91′2′092—dc21

   00-009493

Printed in the United States of America

10 9 8 7 6 5 4 3 2 1

**To Our Readers:**
All Internet Addresses in this book were active and appropriate when we went to press. Any comments or suggestions can be sent by e-mail to Comments@enslow.com or to the address on the back cover.

**Photo Credits:** AP Photo/Brett Coomer, p. 45; AP Photo/CP, Paul Chiasson, p. 14; AP Photo/Dan Loh, p. 40; AP Photo/Eric Draper, p. 9; AP Photo/Mark Lennihan, p. 51; AP Photo/Paul Chiasson, p. 24; AP Photo/Suzanne Tobias, p. 59; Associated Press, AP, pp. 35, 67, 70, 73, 75, 86, 89.

**Cover Photo:** AP Photo/Eric Draper

# Contents

# Chapter 1

# Olympic Wondergirl

As Tara Lipinski stood next to 516-pound sumo wrestler Akebono, a strange sensation came over the four-foot eleven-inch Olympian—fear.

This fifteen-year-old girl, who could launch herself into the air and do three complete spins as if it were something natural, was scared? The Tara Lipinski who won the World Figure Skating Championships on her second try was afraid? The girl, who thought nothing of setting new goals every year, and then surpassing them, was frightened?

"He was so BIG!" Lipinski said of her meeting with the huge sumo superstar at the White Ring arena in Nagano, Japan, where she would compete in the Olympics a few days later. "I looked up at him and just took a deep breath. I wondered if this [meeting him] was such a smart thing to do."[1]

Lipinski then laughed that charming giggle of hers as she thought about how silly that scene was, even as Akebono was saying, "Ah, it's beauty and the beast."

"But I'm glad I did it [posed for photos with Akebono]," she added. "I'm happy about everything in Nagano."[2]

And why not? The 1998 Winter Olympics were a grand experience for Lipinski. While her American teammates, Michelle Kwan and Nicole Bobek, would be arriving late in Japan with hardly any time to enjoy the Olympic festivities, Lipinski was everywhere.

She lived in the Athletes Village, the area set aside for Olympic athletes to live together. She played video games in the arcade with athletes from Russia, the Czech Republic, and Australia. She went to hockey games and other skating events. She went sightseeing. She marched in the opening ceremonies.

Oh, yes, Tara Lipinski also won the gold medal in the figure skating competition. It was the most prestigious title in women's Olympic sports, and she was the youngest skater to win it.

"It felt almost so impossible to go out there and skate great . . . and be the Olympic champion," she

*Tara Lipinski reacts after completing her gold-medal-winning free skate program at the 1998 Olympics in Nagano, Japan.*

said. "It's so exciting for me to know it wasn't a dream. . . . These days are the best days of my life and I'll always remember them."[3]

Lipinski did not go into the Olympics as the favorite. Although she had won the 1997 United States and world championships, she was the underdog to Michelle Kwan. Kwan beat her at Skate America in their first meeting of the 1997–1998 schedule. Then Kwan was almost perfect in winning again at the U.S. Championships in Philadelphia, Pennsylvania, where Lipinski looked nervous and unsure of herself.

Lipinski had fallen awkwardly in the short program before rallying to finish second in the free skate and earning a spot on the Olympic team that would be competing in Nagano, Japan.

But Lipinski was not feeling any bad vibes when she traveled halfway across the world to do exactly what she had dreamed about since she was two years old. In 1984, playing in front of the television set, she became fascinated with the medals ceremony at the Winter Olympics.

"This is so great," said Lipinski when she arrived at the games. "It's not like any other competition. I've been dreaming of it for so long. It's not like a world championship that you can go to every year. This is a once in a lifetime."[4]

Not that she was ignoring her chores. Each day, Lipinski would practice her routines to music from the film *Anastasia* for her short program, and to "The Rainbow" for her free skate. She and Coach Richard Callaghan would go over each of the jumps and spins and all of the footwork. If Lipinski fell on a certain jump, she would work on it until it was done cleanly. If her spins were a bit off, she would go back out on the ice to perfect them.

Then, without fail, she would stop to talk to the reporters who watched her every move. She chatted about the day ahead or where she had gone the previous day in a friendly manner.

In fact, by the end of the Olympics, most media members were ready to give Tara Lipinski a gold medal, too. "Hey, you guys have been so nice to me," she said one day to the dozen reporters who had followed her entire career. "You're nice people and I like talking to all of you. It's fun."[5]

Taking hold of the entire Olympic experience was, in the end, a huge reason for Tara Lipinski's excellent performance. She fit in from the moment she got to Japan until the day she left.

"It's been a phenomenal experience for her," said her father, Jack. "It's a growing experience, but it's also the ambiance of being there and representing the U.S." Added her mom, Pat,

If she takes nothing else from these games, if she gets nothing, but goes home and knows how to be in unity with people, that's all going to help her in the other world she's going into soon. She's not going to skate forever. She'll go to college, maybe run a company, or be a doctor, whatever. She'll take all this with her, dealing with people from every country. She's learning to communicate with them.[6]

Lipinski also benefited from having one of her closest friends in skating, ice dancer Jessica Joseph, as her roommate. They inspired one another, although Joseph was a little more serious about getting her homework done. Lipinski found plenty of time to eat—pasta, chocolate chip cookies and her favorite dish, ice cream. She likes milkshakes so much that her parents bought her a blender for Christmas one year.

But every day at the Olympics was like Christmas for Lipinski—especially when she marched in the opening ceremonies.

Todd Eldredge, the United States men's champion, who was Lipinski's good friend and trained with her in Detroit, Michigan, remembered his first Olympic experience in 1992 in Albertville, France. He was injured and did not skate well, but he would never forget the opening festivities. "I told Tara that of all the things that happened during the Olympics,

**FACT**

A columnist at Nagano wrote a story saying Tara Lipinski and Todd Eldredge someday might get married. Both skaters laughed loudly when asked about it. But Lipinski's mom said with a smile, "Well, I'd be happy. He's super." Todd Eldredge is eleven years older than Tara Lipinski.

the most memorable for me were marching in with the U.S. team," Eldredge said. "I think she felt the same way when we did it here."[7]

She sure did. "It was almost indescribable," she said.

> I've never been in anything like it, ever. I'm feeling so high, I almost feel like I'm not competing, I'm having so much fun. I had so many thoughts going through my mind, thinking how it would be, and this was finally it. Walking in was the best part, when we came out of the tunnel and they said your country was the best.[8]

It was more than a week after Lipinski arrived in Nagano that she and Michelle Kwan got onto the ice together in a practice session. All the figure skaters from the same nation practice in the same time period, so the stories of the rivalry between Lipinski and Kwan began dominating the news from that first day.

In general, the rivals rarely spoke. They occasionally posed for some team photos, and they talked about jet lag on Kwan's first day in Japan. Otherwise, there was little contact. "We're not the best of friends," Kwan said, "but I think we have a friendly relationship."[9]

Both skaters were practicing well as the short

*Stories of the rivalry between Michelle Kwan (left) and Tara Lipinski (right) began dominating Olympic news once the two competitors arrived in Nagano, Japan.*

program approached. Lipinski changed her routine by staying in a hotel with her parents the night before the event, trying to get more rest. She skated early and nailed everything to take the lead in the short program, worth one third of the total score. But when Michelle Kwan was even better about an hour later, the standings showed Kwan first and Lipinski second heading into the free skate two nights later.

Even though she was in second place, Lipinski was gushing over her performance. "I was so excited because it's the Olympics," she said. "It only comes every four years. You don't know how many you'll be in. It was my chance and I proved to everyone that I can handle all the pressure."[10]

> I thought I did a great job. Not even technically, I mean emotionally it was the best moment. I just felt like crying when I did everything. It was that happiness that you get every once in a while. I can't even describe the feeling. It's that feeling that it seems so hard at the moment, and when you do it, it's like a miracle.[11]

Still, she would have to be even better for the free skate. Lipinski knew how good Kwan could be. She had seen it at Skate America and at nationals. In fact, Lipinski liked having such a strong rival. "It's good to have someone pushing you, because it makes you work hard to be better," Lipinski said. "It's another challenge for you."[12]

Lipinski did not seem nervous at her workouts leading into the free skate (also known as the long program). Neither did Kwan. They appeared to know that nobody else in the field could come close to them. Certainly not Nicole Bobek, who fell several times during her short program and was in seventeenth place, ending hopes for American women skaters to take home the gold, silver, and bronze medals. No, it would be Tara Lipinski versus Michelle Kwan for the gold medal.

Kwan would skate first in the final group of six skaters. Lipinski would be the next-to-last skater. Usually, skating later provides a slight advantage. Judges generally give earlier competitors slightly lower marks to leave room for a later performer who may do better. This is not a steadfast rule, and Lipinski was not relying on it.

"There's only one thing I can count on, and that's trying my best," she said.[13]

Kwan, whose last free skate was rewarded with perfect marks of 6.0 at the U.S. Championships in Philadelphia, was not nearly as strong this time. Her routine lacked fire and emotion. Although Kwan did everything in her program, it was not spectacular.

"It seemed like I was in my own world," Kwan

**FACT**

Among the necklace charms Tara likes to wear is one she received from her Uncle Phil that has a skate with "Thumbs Up" written on it. She considers that to be her luckiest piece of jewelry.

said. "I didn't open up and let myself go." Kwan had provided an opening, and Tara Lipinski flew through it.[14]

Lipinski hit every jump perfectly, including a triple loop-triple loop combination that no other skater even tried. Her spins were fast and tight. Her footwork was brilliant. She was in time with the music from beginning to end of the magical four-minute program.

After she finished the last spin, Lipinski sprinted to center ice to take her bows, her mouth wide open in ecstasy. She stamped her feet, threw kisses to the cheering crowd, then left the ice to await the marks.

No matter what the judges said, though, she knew she had done her absolute best. The judges agreed, and when she realized the gold was hers, Lipinski did a happy little dance. "There is nothing that could be better for me," she said breathlessly just moments later. "Anything that goes on in the future, I will be so content with what I have done."[15]

# Chapter 2

# Starting Out

**F**lowers and ribbons. Those were the things Tara Lipinski wanted out of life. As a two year old, Tara was playing in front of the television when the Olympics came on. She looked up and saw a medals presentation. She does not remember for what sport.

When the athletes received their medals—and flowers and ribbons—Tara tipped over the large plastic tubs that held all of her toys. She stood on top of the containers, pretending they were medals stands.

Pat Lipinski, Tara's mom, tied a ribbon around Tara's neck and handed her some flowers. But Pat Lipinski could not have realized that a future Olympic champion had just gotten her first taste of inspiration.

The Lipinskis lived in New Jersey then, and Tara was such an energetic little girl that her mother always had to find something to keep her occupied. The first activity they came up with was roller-skating.

A local skating rink offered a free stuffed bear if a young person signed up for lessons. Pat Lipinski signed up three-year-old Tara.

"Tara didn't like it at all at first," said Pat Lipinski.

> She thought the skates were ugly and she wouldn't put them on until another little girl came over with her skates on. When Tara saw that, she put on the skates and they went out on the rink.[1]

Soon, Tara was asking her parents for more skating time. She appeared in a Christmas show, performing to "Grandma Got Run Over by a Reindeer"—she played a reindeer. Then she began taking private lessons.

From one day a week, she progressed to taking lessons a few days each week, and then to *every* day. She also played some roller hockey with boys, mainly because she was a better skater than most of the other kids at the rink. But hockey was a bit too rough, so she stuck to roller figure skating.

"There were some competitions we went to

**FACT**

Tara Lipinski has many heroes, including Michael Jordan, Wayne Gretzky, Scott Hamilton and "anyone who went to the Olympics." "It's important to have role models, people you look up to who inspire you," she said. "It makes you want something even more."

when we had to get up in the middle of the night and drive to the rinks," Pat Lipinski recalled. "That didn't bother Tara at all, especially when she began winning medals and trophies."[2]

But roller-skating is not an Olympic sport. Several people, seeing how well Tara skated on wheels, suggested she try ice-skating.

Tara's parents were convinced she would not like ice-skating. Pat Lipinski expected Tara to complain about the cold and how uncomfortable it was when she fell on the ice. Indeed, Tara did hate getting wet when she fell. She missed the warm comfort of the roller rink. Initially, she could not figure out how to stand on blades, let alone how to glide around the ice. "We even have videos of Tara's first time on the ice," said her dad. Her mother added, "We thought she was ready to quit. We offered to take her for hot chocolate."[3]

Pat and Jack Lipinski left the ice for a short break, but six-year-old Tara had other ideas. She insisted on staying on the ice, trying to master this strange new way of skating. When her parents returned, Tara was gliding around like a veteran.

"She took everything she had learned in roller skating and applied it to the ice," Pat Lipinski said. "We were kind of amazed."[4]

It was just the beginning of an amazing journey

that took the Lipinskis to the University of Delaware, about one hour's drive away. Tara took lessons there with Coach Scott Gregory, a former ice dance champion for the United States. Lipinski quickly learned the simpler jumps and spins, and soon was entering local competitions.

But she had not given up roller-skating, and put on some sort of skates every day of the week. All of the Lipinskis knew that could not last.

Making the situation more difficult was her dad's promotion at work, which forced the family to move to Texas. It was hard for the fourth grader to adjust to a new home in a new place. As if things were not hectic enough—some days, Tara did her homework and ate meals in the car on the way to and from practice. Her parents made the adjustment a bit easier when they bought Tara a horse for Christmas, an Arabian she named Moonray.

Tara also had decided to stick to ice-skating and drop roller-skating. She began taking lessons with Megan Faulkner in Texas, and spent one summer back in Delaware working with Jeff DiGregorio. Like Gregory, they are world-class coaches.

DiGregorio felt it best if Tara moved back to Delaware, a strong figure skating area; Texas is hardly that. It was a very tough decision. Jack Lipinski needed to remain in Texas for his job. Tara's skating would improve the most if she went to Delaware.

Finally, the Lipinskis decided to live in separate places. Tara's dad would stay in Texas, while Tara and her mom would go to Delaware. "We knew it [the decision to move] would come at some time," Pat Lipinski said. "If Tara was going to make progress in skating, this was what we needed to do. It wasn't easy, but we felt it was necessary."[5]

The separation made both Tara and her mom homesick. It was also very expensive: They had to rent an apartment in Delaware; pay for ice time and skating lessons; get a private tutor for Tara's school-work (which she has had since sixth grade); and pay for telephone calls to Texas.

But all of the sacrifices and expenses began paying off. Tara soared through the various levels of the sport, easily passing tests through the juvenile and intermediate ranks. By 1994, DiGregorio believed she was a future champion for the United States, maybe even an Olympian.

Tara would be competing on the novice level at nationals, to be held in Detroit. They were also the Olympic trials for the U.S. skating team.

Lipinski finished second at nationals after Coach Faulkner arranged for her to spend a few days training at the Detroit Skating Club. While she was there,

*Tara Lipinski moved quickly and easily through the various levels of ice skating competitions.*

Richard Callaghan, one of America's top coaches, watched her.

Callaghan told Lipinski he liked how hard she worked and how there was no nonsense in her training. She thanked him, never realizing that in another year, he would be her coach.

Winning the silver medal at novice level meant Lipinski was ready for junior competition, the final step before seniors. Her mom did not worry that success was coming too fast for Tara—not when her daughter was having such a good time on and off the ice.

"If she's not baking a cake, she's out with her girlfriends," Pat said. "She's to the movies. She's to the mall, she's shopping. She rides bicycles, plays tennis, goes horseback riding. She really has a full life. It's not just skating. It's intensified around it."[6]

Tara's first truly big test would be at the 1994 United States Olympic Festival in St. Louis, Missouri. The Olympic Festival was an event for America's young athletes on their way up. Tara would stay in the Athletes Village with other competitors from all different sports.

For the first time, she would compete in a large arena and before a big crowd, with television coverage and lots of attention. She loved it. "I think what made the Festival so great was all of these people kind of discovered who I was and saw my skating," she said. "And when I won, I kind of proved to myself I could be good at this."[7]

Tara Lipinski was not just good, she was very good. Not only did she win the gold medal, she was also awarded the Mary Lou Retton Award for the best performance at the festival. At twelve years old, Lipinski was the youngest Olympic Festival gold medal winner.

She took and passed her junior level test. That October, Lipinski was sent to Germany to skate in her first international competition, the Blue Swords Trophy. It was a minor event, but she won. For the first time, skaters and officials in another country took notice of this tiny American whose abilities had earned her the nickname "jumping bean."

A few weeks later, Lipinski flew across the Atlantic Ocean again. This time, it was to take part in a big international event, the World Junior Championships, held in Budapest, Hungary, on Thanksgiving weekend.

Lipinski spent part of her time in Budapest shopping, and part of it enjoying the wonderful Hungarian food, but she missed having a turkey dinner for Thanksgiving. She spent the rest of her trip training and competing, and finished an impressive fourth.

## FACT

Tara Lipinski was not actually invited to the 1994 United States Olympic Festival in St. Louis, Missouri. She was an alternate who went to the event when another skater dropped out. She earned the gold medal at twelve years old—as the youngest winner at any Olympic Festival.

Then it was on to the United States Junior Championships in Providence, Rhode Island, where Tara Lipinski no longer was a nobody.

As she looked back on the first twelve and a half years of her life, she had this to say:

> You have to sacrifice some things. Like, I'm not going to school, but I'm still getting a great education. And I have all my friends. I would never want to give up this experience, as much as I love going in front of all the people and doing the best that I can. I hope skating will be in my life for a very, very long time . . . skating will always be a part of my life.[8]

# Chapter 3

# The Rivalry Begins

Through the years, figure skating has had it share of rivalries. Recently, those head-to-head battles have become front-page sports news.

Katarina Witt and Debi Thomas became the "Dueling Carmens" when they both performed free skate routines from that opera during the 1988 Olympics. At those same games came the "Battle of the Brians," between American champion Brian Boitano and Canadian star Brian Orser, good friends and great competitors.

Has any event been more hyped than the meeting of Tonya Harding and Nancy Kerrigan in 1994 at the Lillehammer Olympics? Nancy Kerrigan won silver and Tonya Harding finished eighth before being banned from the sport for her part in a plot to injure Kerrigan. An associate of Harding's hit Kerrigan in the knee just before she was to compete in the United States Championships. It was an unsuccessful attempt to keep Kerrigan from competing in the Olympics.

Never, though, had there been such a fierce rivalry among such young performers as there was between Tara Lipinski and Michelle Kwan. The merits of each performer are intensely debated by legions of adoring fans.

While Kwan is the "old lady" of the duo, she is only two years older than Lipinski. Both were phenoms at an early age, finding the spotlight even before their twelfth birthdays.

From 1995 through the 1998 Olympics, they were the centerpieces of American women's figure skating—even if they were not quite women yet.

Tara Lipinski's introduction to the national media came at the 1994 United States Olympic Festival. But the first real look at Lipinski as a refreshing personality came at nationals in Providence, Rhode Island, the following February.

By then, there were comparisons, for both young skaters had won Festival crowns. "It's not the height of their career and they're not peaking," veteran coach Kathy Casey said. "However, it's been a great launching block for people such as Tara Lipinski and Michelle Kwan. They won this competition and it vaulted them into a different league."[1]

Lipinski was competing in the junior league in Providence, while Kwan was favored in seniors. They would not face each other in competition. They did, however, share the same stage as reporters flocked to speak with them at practices or during news conferences.

Kwan talked about not being bothered by the pressure of people saying she was the next great American figure skater. She had been an alternate for the 1994 Olympics after the Tonya Harding and Nancy Kerrigan incident, but she did not get to skate in the games. She did, though, become a household name.

Lipinski was just as strongly favored in juniors as Kwan was in seniors. And she was excited about her chances. "I just landed my first triple flip and I want to do it in a competition," she said. "I can't wait to try it."[2]

There did not seem to be anything that could tone down Lipinski's enthusiasm. Everything about her life made her smile. "It's a lot of fun," she said. "Going to different countries, I like the celebrity, all the cameras and anything like that. After I'm done competing, I like doing press conferences and all."[3]

What she could not have liked was losing. Nor could Kwan. Neither skater lived up to expectations

**FACT**

Nobody loves dogs more than Tara Lipinski. She has had a bunch of pets, including Mischief, Camelot, Lancelot, Brandy, and Coco. When she was moving around so much, Lipinski had dogs back home in Texas and with her wherever she lived. She also owned a white Arabian horse named Moonray.

in Providence. Kwan struggled in the short program, but felt confident as she stood third. "Top three, you're still able to be first," Kwan said. "You just have to work hard at it."[4] She worked hard, as always, but still fell short of Nicole Bobek. Maybe, at fourteen years old, it just was not her time.

"I don't feel the pressure got to me," said Kwan. "Going into it, I felt really confident and knew I could get through the program. I was really proud. I don't really care about overall standing."[5]

And Lipinski? She also came in second in her event, behind Sydne Vogel. But she nailed the triple flip. "That is my hardest triple," she admitted. "I had confidence in doing it, because I did it in warm-ups. But I was still thinking about it. In any competition, there is one jump that's hard and you usually think about it."[6]

As for a rematch? "I'll beat her next year," Lipinski said with a smile.[7] (And she did beat her.) She was talking about Vogel, but she could have meant Kwan. That was who her true rival would become.

That fall, Lipinski was again entered in the World Junior Championships, but she finished a disappointing fifth. The family decided it was time to thank Jeff DiGregorio for his help in getting Lipinski to this high level and to find a new coach with more international experience. After talking to several top instructors, Lipinski's mom moved to Detroit so her daughter could train with Richard Callaghan.

That all took place only a few weeks before the 1995 United States Championships. It sounds silly, but fifteen-year-old Kwan and thirteen-year-old Lipinski would be the headliners of *senior* women's skating.

Kwan and Lipinski were aware of each other's skating reputations, but their paths rarely crossed. There was no opportunity for them to become friends. Their homes were in different parts of the United States, and, until 1996, they were skating at different levels. That meant even if they were scheduled to compete at the same rink, they did not practice at the same time.

Tara and Pat Lipinski had met Frank Carroll, who coaches Kwan and helped Linda Fratianne win an Olympic silver medal in 1980. When the Lipinskis went looking for a world-class coach to guide Tara's career, they might have considered Carroll had he not been Kwan's coach.

Instead, they turned to Richard Callaghan, who was on a hot streak. Callaghan's top two students, Todd Eldredge and Nicole Bobek, had won the 1995 National Championships. For Eldredge, it was his third title; he would win five. For Bobek, who had been an underachiever, it was her first crown, but she soon left Callaghan.

Callaghan and Carroll had something of a friendly rivalry, too. In the early 1990s, the top two American skaters were Eldredge, trained by Callaghan, and Christopher Bowman, who worked with Carroll. "There is a very strong mutual respect there," Carroll said. "I believe Richard is one of the finest coaches anywhere, and the results prove it."[8]

Added Callaghan, "What Frank has done as a coach in his career is what all of us in the business would like to do. He has a long history of success, and he and Michelle have been great for figure skating. You have to congratulate and applaud Frank for what he has done in the sport and for the sport."[9]

Tara and Pat Lipinski moved into a new place in suburban Detroit while Jack Lipinski once again remained behind in Texas to work at his job and tend to the Lipinskis' home and dogs.

Tara Lipinski loved the Detroit Skating Club where Callaghan coached. It is a huge building with two world-class rinks and a strong figure skating program. And in Todd Eldredge, she discovered a sort of big brother. Whenever she had a question about skating at the highest level, she could turn to Eldredge, who is nearly eleven years older than she.

*With the help of Coach Callaghan, Tara Lipinski worked hard and gained a lot of confidence in her work.*

She could also get advice on how best to work with Callaghan, or just talk.

"Tara has a lot of confidence," Eldredge said. "She looks at herself as someone who will work hard to get anything done, and that anything is possible."[10] Including beating Kwan in their first major face-off? Sure, why not?

Actually, Lipinski could find plenty of reasons why not. As she wrote in her book, *Triumph on Ice*, Lipinski was sure nationals would be a disaster, that she was in over her head against the likes of Michelle Kwan, Nicole Bobek, and Tonia Kwiatkowski who was competing before Tara had even begun skating.

Lipinski admitted to being nervous and, for the first time in a very long while, thinking she could not win a medal.

The national championships were in San Jose, California. They would become most memorable because local skater Rudy Galindo, who had been in seniors for more than a decade, then quit for a year, made a comeback—and won. There were cheers and tears everywhere when Galindo outskated Eldredge in one of the biggest upsets in American figure skating history.

Could Lipinski match that? Was it her time to become a champion, to beat Kwan, her new rival, to the top? Not quite.

Kwan skated beautifully in both the short program and the free skate to easily win. As predicted in 1994 by just about everyone in the sport, Kwan was a champion. But Tara Lipinski was not far behind. Kwiatkowski was second, and along with Kwan, earned a spot on the United States team for the World Championships a month later. Lipinski came in third; Bobek, the defending champion, withdrew just before the free skate with an ankle injury.

Bobek asked the United States Figure Skating Association to give her a place on the world team. That would mean bumping Lipinski, and many people thought that would happen. It was rare when a defending United States champion dropped out of nationals and then was not permitted to go to worlds. But a committee picked Lipinski to go to Edmonton, Canada, for worlds, making Bobek the alternate.

"I think Tara has definitely earned the right," Callaghan said.[11]

While Lipinski still needed lots of work on her artistry, her jumps were brilliant. She was hitting them regularly, and with improvement in her presentation, Lipinski very soon could challenge Kwan.

"I think if she skated as well as she did tonight," Callaghan said after the San Jose event, "she would do exceptionally well at worlds."[12]

Ah, the World Championships. Now this would

be special. For one thing, it would be the first time Kwan and Lipinski would be teammates. For another, so many of Lipinski's skating dreams revolved around international events such as worlds and the Olympics.

Midori Ito of Japan, the 1989 world champion and the first woman to do a triple axel jump—the hardest of all triples—in competition, was in Lipinski's practice group. Lipinski idolized Midori Ito. "To see a world-class skater like her out there— at my practice, I was watching her," said Lipinski. "I know she was second at the [1992] Olympics and is really a great skater, with her jumps and her speed."[13]

That was the only hint Lipinski was even the slightest bit in awe of where she was. Her confidence was high. "This is amazing and really exciting," she said. "I love to skate for the people and have them clap. I get a lot of attention and I like it."[14]

She would not like her early performance at worlds. Although Lipinski was second to Ito in her qualifying round, she had a disastrous short program. Ito skated one spot in front of Lipinski in the short and did not do well, either. Lipinski heard Ito's marks and got distracted because they were low. She started thinking about winning instead of thinking about skating her best.

And she skated her worst. She fell on her second jump. She made mistakes on her third jump. She dropped all the way to twenty-third place out of thirty skaters. She was lucky to qualify for the free skate at all.

Meanwhile, Michelle Kwan was right at the top. And she would stay there, adding her first world title to her first United States crown.

Lipinski was not anywhere near Kwan's level, and unless she could pull herself together, she could forget about being mentioned in the same breath with Kwan. The rivalry would be over before it ever really began. But anyone who knows Tara Lipinski understands she is not a quitter. She was angry with herself for not concentrating on her job. She knew what to do.

So, out onto the ice she went. At thirteen years old, the youngest skater in the World Championships, Lipinski performed her free skate routine like a veteran. She hit every element. She landed seven triple jumps, including the difficult triple Salchow-triple-toe loop combination.

From that lowly twenty-third place, she moved all the way up to fifteenth place overall by finishing eleventh in the free skate, which is worth two thirds

*Tara Lipinski did not perform well at the World Championships. She fell on her second jump, and made mistakes on her third jump.*

of the total score. She was not as high in the rankings as she originally wanted to be, but she had improved.

"I think I proved to myself that I can come back when I have to," she said. "I didn't let myself get down over what happened. I made sure I used it to help me skate better."[15]

And when Todd Eldredge won the men's title, Tara Lipinski could leave Edmonton smiling.

# Chapter 4

# American Champ, World Champ

**T**ara Lipinski was not a star yet, or even a champion. But everything was in place for her to reach the top. Still, as a fourteen-year-old, she could not expect to begin collecting gold medals quite yet. In swimming or gymnastics, fourteen is a prime age for female athletes. In figure skating, though, maturity and reputation are important in the judges' minds. At such a young age and with such a short career behind her, Lipinski remained a longshot to win a championship heading into the 1996–97 skating season.

Her season began at Skate Canada in Kitchener, where one judge actually mistook the four-foot eight-inch, seventy-pound Lipinski for a flower girl. Armed with two new programs, Lipinski finished second. For the first time as a senior skater, she had won a medal at an international event, finishing behind Russia's Irina Slutskaya, who was ranked third in the world.

Lipinski also won $18,000—Olympic-eligible skaters are allowed to earn money for their expenses when they compete in events approved by the International Skating Union.

Next up was the Lalique Trophee in Paris, France, where Lipinski would face Michelle Kwan. In order to skate on Kwan's level, Lipinski had to improve her artistry. Her family hired Sandra Bezic, a world-famous choreographer who had put together artistic programs for such champions as Brian Boitano, Katarina Witt, Brian Orser, and Kurt Browning.

"I knew Sandra was an expert on what you need to become an artist on the ice," Lipinski said. "We listened to music together and came up with a program to go with the music. Then she helped me to feel the music and interpret it."[1]

Skating to music from the movie *Sense and Sensibility*, Tara Lipinski became more expressive. She no longer was a jumping jack who did very little between her triple Lutzes and loops. She did not just skate, she performed.

Everyone in the skating world began noticing.

*Tara Lipinski autographs a teddy bear for a fan. People all over began to take notice of Lipinski as her performances began to improve.*

"Tara is showing a little bit of everything," Bezic said. "She has the jumps and now she has the look and the artistic impression to go with it."[2]

She also had a look of confusion on her face during the long program at Lalique, however. After a strong short program, Lipinski "got lost" during her free skate. She completed a spin and was unsure where she was on the ice—and began skating in the wrong direction.

Coach Callaghan told Lipinski it was a good lesson. She needed to get familiar with every rink and arena in which she skated.

Lipinski finished third at Lalique, behind Kwan and Russian star Maria Butyrskaya. And Paris was a great deal of fun for Lipinski, who had time to play tourist and see the Eiffel Tower and Notre Dame Cathedral. Thanks to skating, she was visiting the places that she had dreamed of seeing when she was a little girl.

Before Lipinski headed home to prepare for the national championships, the United States Skating Federation contacted her. They wanted to know if she could go to the Nations Cup the following week in Germany. An American skater had withdrawn and there was an opening.

Never one to back off a challenge or a chance to skate, Lipinski said yes. It was not a very smart decision, however: Competing for the third straight week, she was too tired to be at her best. Although Lipinski finished second to Slutskaya, her programs were filled with errors. It was very surprising that three of the seven judges placed her first.

More experienced, and with three senior international medals in her collection, Lipinski went back to Detroit to work. Callaghan asked her to look forward and try something no other skater in the world did: a triple loop-triple loop combination.

Lipinski already had the triple Salchow-triple loop combo down. But this was more difficult.

The coach knew she could do it if she applied herself, because Lipinski always mastered her jumps once she spent time on them. To have any chance to beat Kwan at nationals or worlds, Lipinski would need high technical marks.

"I tried to make Tara understand that while she was making great improvement with her artistry, if she was technically superior to the other skaters, it could give her an edge," Callaghan said. "A triple loop-triple loop is a difficult combination, but she rotates quickly enough to do it. And she is very good at landing and taking off from the [blade] edge. I admit I didn't know how long it might take for her to do the combination."[3]

It would only take one attempt. On her first try,

Tara Lipinski smoothly landed the triple loop-triple loop. A smile lit up her face. She tried it again—and fell. After a few more tries, she could not do both jumps. She was off-balance after the first triple loop. After working with Callaghan for several hours, Lipinski regularly began hitting the combination. Eventually, it would become the centerpiece of her programs.

First, though, she had to land it in a competition. Not wanting to test it at nationals, Lipinski chose to try the combination at the United States Postal Service Team Pro-Am in Philadelphia.

Lipinski was hardly the biggest star there— Michelle Kwan and Dorothy Hamill were on her team, while Todd Eldredge, Paul Wylie, and Rosalynn Sumners were on the other squad. But Lipinski got most of the attention when she nailed the triple loop-triple loop perfectly. She was ready for nationals.

When she arrived in Nashville for nationals, Tara Lipinski admitted she had her eyes, not on first place, but on any spot in the top three, so she could make the United States team for worlds again. Beating Kwan was not the main focus. "I was really excited and surprised to be on the world team last year," Lipinski said. "I had to work hard and to concentrate on two clean programs for this year to stay there."[4]

Lipinski placed second to Kwan in the short program, overcoming a case of nerves before she skated. She always gets excited about competitions, but she admitted to being extra nervous until speaking with Callaghan and gymnastics coach Bela Karolyi, who gave her a pep talk on the telephone.

Before the free skate the next day, Lipinski spoke with Eldredge, who won his fourth national championship in Nashville. They had become good friends from all the practice sessions working with Callaghan and from traveling to the same competitions.

Eldredge told her to have faith in her skills and to just go out and do what she was trained to do. Callaghan told her the same thing. It would have been easy to get nervous all over again, because she drew the last skating spot, something few skaters enjoy.

Instead, it was Michelle Kwan who had problems with the pressure. She fell three times in her long program—more than she usually fell in a season.

"I guess I wasn't concentrating," Kwan said. "I guess I panicked in the middle of my performance after the slip. It was just mind games and I got scared in the middle."[5]

Lipinski was standing by the ice when the

judges' marks for Kwan came on the scoreboard. The crowd began booing, and Callaghan told Lipinski not to worry, that the booing was for the marks. Lipinski also knew what such low marks meant: If she skated her best, if she hit everything, she could win.

So what did Tara Lipinski do? She skated her best. She hit everything. She won, becoming the youngest U.S. champion.

"It was so exciting, just skating a good program," Lipinski said.

> And after the second marks came, that's when I actually knew. Just being a champion, no matter what the age, is great. I'm on a different wave length tonight, something high. This is perfect.[6]

Her national championship came long before anyone expected it. But Lipinski had earned it by jumping cleaner and skating more artistically than anyone else. Now, she had to prove it was no fluke.

But first, she taped an appearance on *Late Night with David Letterman*. She was on *Good Morning America* and *This Morning*. She visited the studio of famous fashion designer Donna Karan, who supplies gear for the United States skating team.

Just two weeks later, she and Kwan met again, at

*Tara Lipinski and Boyz II Men present the award for Best Pop Album at the 40th annual Grammy Awards.*

the Champions Series Finals in Hamilton, Canada. This time, top Europeans would be in the event.

Again, Lipinski was the best, beating Kwan and Slutskaya. She was not perfect, as she had been at nationals, however. Lipinski nearly crashed into the sideboards after missing a double axel. She just shrugged it off and did not miss a trick the rest of the way.

"This was nice and more experience for me, which is good," she said. "So when I go to worlds, I'll have more confidence in myself, because I've done it and this was a good warm-up."[7]

Added Callaghan, "Nothing bothers Tara. She missed an element, she forgot about it and did the rest of her work."[8]

Her biggest chore was yet to come. Having beaten Kwan twice in a row and conquered some of the top international stars in Hamilton, the next step was the World Championships in Lausanne, Switzerland.

At worlds, there are three performances: qualifying, the short program, and the free skate. In qualifying, the skaters performed their long programs. In 1997, as long as a skater placed high enough to qualify for the short program, the position they finished in was not important. Most skaters held back in qualifying and did not bother to give it their all.

Not Lipinski. Even as the older competitors were struggling and taking it easy, she tried and nailed everything to lead her qualifying group. That boosted her confidence heading into the short program, where one mistake can be disastrous. In the two-minute forty-second program, there are eight required elements. Should a skater skip an element or have problems with one, the judges automatically deduct points.

Although the short program is worth just one third of the total score, it can eliminate a contender if she skates poorly.

Lipinski was uncomfortable with the three-day break between qualifying and the short program. She was rolling and wanted to get right back on the ice.

By the morning of her short program, her nervousness had returned. Even worse, she learned that Carlo Fassi had died unexpectedly. Fassi was one of the world's most famous skating coaches. He was in Lausanne training Nicole Bobek, who had earned the last spot on the American team by finishing third at nationals in Nashville. Lipinski had been on the ice that morning and had seen Fassi working with Bobek just a short time before his heart attack.

**FACT**

Tara Lipinski did not know Carlo Fassi well, but she knew the man who died during the 1997 World Championships was a great coach. Fassi had worked with Peggy Fleming and Dorothy Hamill, who both won Olympic gold medals, and was coaching 1995 United States champion Nicole Bobek when he died.

The whole skating world was shocked and saddened to learn of his death.

Lipinski was sad, but she knew she could not let her mood affect her skating. Nor could she let the fact that she had drawn the last spot in the skating order affect her.

So she did what she does best: She responded to a challenge. Lipinski hit everything and won the short program at worlds, just one year after she had finished twenty-third in it.

"It felt great being able to do a clean short this year," Lipinski said. "It gave me a lot of confidence."[9]

Another boost of confidence came when she saw the standings. Kwan had fallen and was fourth; Slutskaya was way down in sixth.

Lipinski was four minutes from becoming the youngest Women's World Champion ever. Because she was so far ahead, Lipinski did not even have to win the free skate to beat her American rival, Michelle Kwan.

"I never expected it. Especially not this year," she said. "It's a big shock. But I love it."[10]

She loved it even more when she skated so well in the free skate that the judges awarded her nothing but 5.8s and 5.9s out of a possible 6.0. She even received a higher mark in artistry than in technique from the Polish judge.

Although Kwan finally "got it together" and won the free skate, Lipinski was second, good enough to keep Lipinski in first overall and give her the World Championship.

At fourteen years, nine months, and twelve days old, she was thirty-two days younger than Sonja Henie was when the Norwegian won the first of her ten world titles in 1927. Even better, the Olympics were coming up in eleven months. Tara Lipinski would be going to the Olympics as the reigning World Champion. Michelle Kwan would be going as the challenger.

"We're both young," Kwan said. "I don't know how long she intends to be skating. But I'll be there, always."[11]

**FACT**

Beginning in 1996, Lipinski worked with Marina Sheffer, a ballet teacher. She began taking ballet lessons when she was seven years old, and Sheffer's ability to make her more expressive and artistic on the ice helped her win her first major championships.

# Chapter 5

# The Olympic Buildup

**H**er first offseason as the world champion was a fun time for Tara Lipinski. She did the things teenage girls usually do—shopping or just hanging out at malls; gossiping about boys; going to the movies; or going on vacation.

She also starred in the Tom Collins Champions on Ice figure skating tour, which featured many of the world's top skaters and lasted for nearly three months.

Lipinski enjoyed being on tour with such greats as Olympic gold medal winners Brian Boitano and Oksana Baiul. She learned from them, and also found that her artistic skating improved simply by performing a showy routine every night.

She chose "Reach," by Gloria Estefan, and skated

to a program put together by former United States ice dance champion Susan Wynne. While Lipinski hardly was the headliner with such skaters as Boitano, Baiul, Nancy Kerrigan, Elvis Stojko, and Todd Eldredge in the show, her routine was very popular with audiences.

But it was not all fun and games for Lipinski. She said:

> All the time, I'd stop and think that the Olympics were coming up. I knew I had to work really hard to make the team; just because you're the world or national champion one year doesn't mean you'll stay up there the next. It's going to be my first Olympics. If I don't do it this time, there's always another one. It'd be great to win it.
>
> But you don't want to just think about that, because that's not what skating is to me. You want to have fun with it and get the experience and be there and enjoy skating at that level.[1]

Lipinski knew she faced a major challenge from Michelle Kwan, her American rival, as well as from the strong Russian and French skaters. She would have liked nothing better than to begin the Olympic buildup with a first-place finish at Skate America.

And she had the home-ice advantage for that event, which was held in Detroit at the end of

*Tara Lipinski skates at Rockefeller Plaza ice rink in New York after winning the gold medal at the Olympics. Before she could get there, though, she needed to perfect her routines.*

October 1997. It was the first important international competition heading toward the Nagano Games.

"For Tara, this is the beginning of a new season, with new material and jumps," coach Richard Callaghan said.

> It's kind of a stepping stone to the national championships and the Olympics. I think Tara has developed over the last year. Performing on tour in the springtime and being around the older performers, she was able to choose from what they did and incorporate it into what she does.

"Every time they come in, we have something they need to work on that day," added Callaghan, who also coached Eldredge at the Detroit Skating Club.

> We don't work on it for the Olympics. We work on it just to get it better. I don't want them thinking about the Olympics. I want them thinking about day-to-day enjoyment of the skating and being prepared.[2]

Lipinski tried to play down the rivalry with Kwan, even while the media was playing it up. "We're friends off the ice," Lipinski said. "We talk in the locker room. There's nothing going on. On the ice, she is just like any other competitor. We are trying for the same thing."[3]

Kwan got the edge this time by winning Skate

America. She was first in the short program. When Lipinski fell on a triple Lutz in the free skate while Kwan's routine was error-free and more artistic, the judges' decision was easy.

"The mistake I made was not a big deal," Lipinski said after finishing second. "I'm glad it didn't come from doubting myself. Last year, I was in the same position in my first three internationals. It gives me something to work for and keep motivated."[4]

Lipinski kept busy, something Kwan could not do after suffering a stress fracture in her foot. Kwan would be sidelined until nationals, while Lipinski headed to Paris for the Lalique Trophee.

In Paris, Lipinski was a heavy favorite against a weak field that did not include anyone who had beaten her recently. But she was weakened by a cold. After winning the short program easily, she made several mistakes in the free skate.

That was enough for France's Laetitia Hubert to win, with Lipinski finishing second. Losing to Kwan was one thing. But coming in behind Hubert, whose best finish in World Championships had been fourth, was another.

Lipinski was very disappointed with her performance. She cut down a triple Lutz to a double, made a triple loop a single, and was unable to do any triple-triple combinations. After ending the previous

**FACT**

Before the 1996 Atlanta Olympics, Tara Lipinski helped her friend, and gymnast, Dominique Moceanu, get psyched up for the Games. But when a bomb exploded in Atlanta's Centennial Park during the Olympics, the Lipinskis decided not to go watch Moceanu. Instead, Lipinski watched the women of the United States on television as they won the gold medal.

season with her three biggest victories, she now had a two-event streak of runner-up results.

"This year I haven't had the experience of moving up like I did last year," Lipinski said. "I never expected this year to win everything. I knew I couldn't. I didn't want to. Once you are world champion, there is a little more pressure to stay on top."[5]

Lipinski's mini-slump did not affect her popularity. In fact, at the wise old age of fifteen, she was already a role model for plenty of girls just starting out in sports.

Lipinski heard about Danielle Winningham, a six-year-old in West Virginia who was inspired to become a figure skater when she saw Lipinski performing on television. As a first grader, Winningham already had mastered spinning and was working on jumps.

"I want to be like Tara Lipinski, because she wins everything," Danielle said.[6]

Well, Lipinski had not been winning lately. So, she headed back to Detroit for some fine-tuning. She needed to be sharper on the ice and more focused off it. While preparing for her next big competition, the Champions Series final in Munich, Germany, Lipinski received a much-needed boost. The United

States Olympic Committee announced she was its Sportswoman of the Year.

At first, she could not believe it, and she asked her mother if it was true. When she was assured that she had in fact joined Scott Hamilton—one of her idols—and Linda Fratianne as the only figure skaters to win the award, Lipinski acted just like a fifteen-year-old should upon hearing such good news; she jumped up and down and shrieked gleefully.

"It's such a great honor," she said.

> Of all the sports people in the U.S., I got picked. It just feels really good. Now I can tell all of my friends. They've all been kind of excited and shocked [about her success]. It's a great thing for me, so they've been really excited.[7]

As the youngest winner of the honor, she had beaten athletes such as soccer great Mia Hamm and track star Marion Jones, the world's fastest woman. The award lifted her spirits as she prepared for the Munich event.

Coach Callaghan was concerned that Lipinski's performances were not being scored fairly by the judges. There was talk that her triple Lutz, which requires a long backward approach while skating on the same edge from which the skater lifts off, was being done improperly. Critics said Tara took off from the other edge of the blade, making the jump a flip instead of a Lutz—or, as it is comically called by skating experts, a "flutz."

"I think this year, Tara, probably being the world champion, is being reviewed a little more," Callaghan said.

> We don't have a problem with that. Quite honestly, I think she's skating way better than last year. Like Tara, I'm a little puzzled by some of the marks. But we're going to deal with it. . . . We are dealing with it.[8]

They dealt with it very well in Munich, where Lipinski returned to the form of the previous year. In her short program, to music from the animated film *Anastasia*, she looked like a little princess. And in the free skate, to "The Rainbow," she soared over the best opposition she would face until the Nagano Olympics two months later.

Lipinski's first victory of the season could be measured by her marks: 5.8s and 5.9s for both technical and artistic presentation in the free skate. No more undermarking.

And no more "flutz," as she perfectly performed the triple Lutz while hitting seven triple jumps, including her two combinations.

If Lipinski needed an extra dose of confidence heading to the United States Championships, she got it in Munich. She also beat the best the world had to offer, making it clear that Lipinski and Kwan would be heavy favorites for the Olympics.

So Tara Lipinski arrived in Philadelphia for nationals not only as the defending national champ, but also very self-assured. She was ready for Kwan—even if she claimed to be thinking about other things.

Lipinski said of Kwan:

> She's like any other competitor to me. I don't have that much time to think about who I'm competing against and how I can beat them. . . . I'd love to win, that'd be a great moment again. But when I go to the rink, I'm just going to think about doing my programs the way I want to do them and making the Olympic team.[9]

Making that team seemed like a sure thing until Lipinski had one of her worst outings in years during the short program. While Kwan was superb, showing no sign of rustiness from her two-month layoff and getting an unheard of seven 6.0s for presentation, Lipinski fell.

On her triple flip, Lipinski's body was so tilted when she jumped that she came crashing down, sprawling across the ice on her backside. She got up and finished her routine, but was almost in tears as she left the rink in fourth place.

Knowing that only three American women

would go to Nagano, Lipinski promised herself she would do something much more impressive in the free skate.

"I just didn't get the lift I needed and I made a mistake," she said of the failed triple flip.

> It wasn't a doubting mistake or a technical problem. It was just a fluke. I would have liked a clean program and to be a little higher, but I'm going to go out Saturday and skate a clean program and get back up there. I've done it before.[10]

And she would do it again. Ignoring the pressure—easily the most severe she had ever been under—Lipinski did it all.

Triple Lutz? No problem, no "flutz."

Triple flip? This time, it was perfect.

Triple loop-triple loop combination? Got it.

Hitting seven triple jumps, floating along the ice smiling and soaring, Lipinski moved up to second place. She was not able to match Kwan's grace and style, as Kwan set a record for 6.0s at nationals with fifteen. But Lipinski showed that the short program was a fluke, and that her championships of the previous year were not.

*Tara Lipinski was going to the Olympics.*

"To come back and do this strongly, with the pressure of making the Olympic team, gives me a lot

Tara Lipinski showed grace and style during the ladies free skating long program in Nagano, Japan. She also showed great determination and hard work to get to the Olympics.

of confidence that, I feel, will carry over," Lipinski said. "I know I can do anything now."[11]

Joining Kwan and Lipinski on the Olympic team was Nicole Bobek, meaning the last three United States champions—Kwan in 1996 and 1998, Lipinski in 1997 and Bobek in 1995—were all going to the Olympics in Nagano, Japan.

"I think it's an awesome team," Lipinski said.[12]

The performances of Kwan for both rounds at nationals and Lipinski in the free skate impressed everyone. As they looked ahead to the Olympics, American skating officials were confident that the gold medal would go to a skater from the United States.

"Definitely, Michelle and Tara have the edge as far as reputation is concerned. They both are world champions, they've both beaten each other off and on over the years," said Frank Carroll, Kwan's coach. "I'm very proud we have two such great skaters coming from the United States."[13]

# Chapter 6

# The Big Decision

Tara Lipinski did not want the magical feeling that the Olympics brought out in her to fade. Hours before CBS televised the women's free skate in the United States on tape, America knew about Lipinski's triumph. The long program, held at night in Nagano, was over in the early morning back home. That meant every news show, from ESPN's *SportsCenter* to NBC's *Today* and ABC's *Good Morning America*, was reporting her victory.

The entire Olympic experience had paid off in gold for Lipinski. She had soaked up everything the games had to offer, and, inspired by it all, she had come through with a magnificent performance. Experts agreed it was the most difficult routine any woman ever skated, highlighted, of course, by her

*Tara Lipinski kissed her gold medal after winning the ladies free skating long program in Nagano, Japan.*

trademark triple loop-triple loop combination. The finishing touch was a triple toe loop-half loop-triple Salchow combo at the very end, which would have been difficult to land even at the beginning of a program, when a skater is fresh.

"I would have stayed out there all night if I could," Lipinski said, clutching and kissing her gold medal. "I'm just going to walk around enjoying being an Olympic champion."[1]

That would not be easy.

While her advisers talked of million-dollar endorsement contracts and television appearances, Lipinski tried to ignore the realities of sports business. She just wanted to be a teenager who happened to be an Olympic gold medal winner, a girl who had fulfilled her dreams.

But everything Tara Lipinski did for the next few years would make news. She would be welcomed home with parades and television interviews. Everyone wanted a piece of the Olympic champion, while the Olympic champion wanted peace.

So Lipinski faded from the spotlight for a few weeks. She was tired—one report said she had mononucleosis, a blood disease that weakens a person for weeks, even months. She missed hanging out with her friends and spending time with her family.

She decided not to go to the World Championships held in Minneapolis a few weeks after the Olympics, disappointing many of her fans. That fueled rumors that she wold turn pro, never to skate in another Olympics—at least not under the current rules. Michelle Kwan, so gracious in defeat at Nagano, became the sport's headliner again by winning worlds.

A few days after that, Lipinski made a big announcement: She would, indeed, turn pro.

"I've been thinking a lot about turning pro, thinking since Nagano, but I really needed time to think more about it," she said.

> I'm really excited about it and a little relieved. I really wanted more time with the family, more time at home. I would love to go to the 2002 Olympics and try to win another gold, but would [feel] almost a little greedy in doing that, especially to my parents, who have given up so much.
>
> Now I'll have four-day weekends and be able to be with my family, because they mean so much to me. I don't want to be 21 and not know my dad.

"I've accomplished my dream," added Lipinski, who was worth approximately $13 million to advertisers after winning her gold medal. "I think I need

*Tara Lipinski reacted with excitement after she saw her scores and realized that she had beaten out Michelle Kwan in their quest for the gold medal.*

to give something back to them, so we can be a family again and really have that connection."

She emphasized,

> I realized after Nagano how important it is to me to be with my mom and dad and be all together and have fun and go out to dinner and really be a family again. I owe that to my parents and myself.[2]

One day later, Tara Lipinski was on the ice in Baltimore, Maryland, with Champions on Ice, her first skating appearance since the Olympics. But it was her participation in "Skate, Rattle 'n Roll," a made-for-television event in Charleston, South Carolina, two weeks later that would have the most impact.

When Lipinski performed in that contest, which was not approved by the International Skating Union, her Olympic eligibility was officially gone.

Coincidentally, just a few days later, she joined her fellow American Olympians from Nagano at the White House. Oddly, it was Kwan, not Lipinski, who was chosen to present President Clinton with a United States team jacket.

That bothered Lipinski's mom, who believed the gold medalist deserved that honor. "Don't you think it's a terrible thing for them to do to poor Tara?" she said, blaming the United States Olympic Committee

*Michelle Kwan (left) silver medalist, Tara Lipinski (center) gold medalist, and China's Lu Chen, bronze medalist stand during the national anthem of the United States during medal ceremonies.*

(USOC). "It's been like this for poor Tara. It's a terrible thing."[3]

USOC spokesman Mike Moran said skier Picabo Street was actually chosen to present the jacket after a vote by the whole Olympic team, but the injured Street could not attend. Moran said Kwan was the second choice in the balloting, and that there was no intended slight of Lipinski.

"It hasn't been necessarily the star of the game," Moran said. "It's not Tara vs. Michelle."[4]

Nor will it likely be again for a while, with Lipinski in the professional ranks and Kwan seeking another Olympic berth in 2002.

Lipinski said:

> I was always the underdog, I felt. If I had been winning, I would have felt I've got to be better and better and better to stay ahead. As the underdog I wanted to be better, but I was out there on the ice myself and never really thought about Michelle.
>
> But having the rivalry we had, as you call it, really did make us both better skaters, and we knew we had to be at our best. For my skating, I never really thought of it that way, other than to push myself to the ultimate. And I don't think I could have done any more.[5]

Tara Lipinski did not exactly become a homebody after turning pro. She traveled throughout the United

**FACT**

Two weeks after winning the gold medal, Tara Lipinski was on stage at Radio City Music Hall with the four members of the music group Boyz II Men. She helped announce that James Taylor had won the Grammy Award for best pop album for "Hourglass." She also got to meet one of her favorite singers, Celine Dion, at the Grammys.

States representing the Boys and Girls Clubs of America and working for such causes as anti-smoking campaigns.

At a Boys and Girls Club in New York City, she was greeted with homemade signs and posters applauding her Olympic success, and chants of "Tara, Tara." She signed autographs for hundreds of youngsters, played Foosball with them, and told them not to lose sight of their own goals.

"My skating club provided a real support system for me, and I'm not sure I could have pulled it off in Nagano without them," Lipinski said. "You have that kind of support in your club here. Everybody here is lucky to have the Boys & Girls Clubs."

Lipinski said afterward, "I hope when they look at whatever they want to do in life, they get inspired by what I've done and my being here and that they set big and great goals and achieve them."[6]

Added Kurt Aschermann, a senior vice president for the Boys and Girls Clubs,

> Tara is an example of exactly what the Boys and Girls Club is telling you. If you have a dream and you can adhere to it—you've got to work at it and go after it—but you can achieve it. She is what the clubs are all about.[7]

Lipinski was not getting much rest, but she was not complaining either. Whether it was the nightly performances of the Champions on Ice tour, her many public appearances, or just filling the role of Olympic champ, she seemed happy.

"I'm busy and sometimes it's hard to keep the days straight," Lipinski said, her eyes sparkling as radiantly as her tour costume. "But this is my favorite part of the year. I'm on tour and hanging out with friends and traveling with them."

> I am so thankful for the Olympics, but I understand the role I have. I always think of [the obligation] being a champion when I get to meet all of these fans. I have to be a great role model. I'll miss it if it ever goes away.[8]

Lipinski would move away from the Champions tour and join Stars on Ice in August, following a well-deserved break that included her usual vacation at Disney World. Scott Hamilton began stars on Ice in 1986, when Tara was four years old, and has become one of the most popular skating shows ever. Hamilton has been one of Lipinski's heroes, as were Kristi Yamaguchi, Rosalynn Sumners, and Ekaterina Gordeeva, all of whom were part of the Stars on Ice tour.

Lipinski also worked closely with Stars on Ice director Sandra Bezic, who put together her Olympic free skate, and Stars choreographer Lea Ann Miller. Lipinski said:

These are my idols and the inspiration for me when I was growing up, and to do a show every night with them will be really cool. It will be so fun doing those group numbers. It's hard work to do solos and can be stressful with the jumps, but in these group numbers, you're out there with people and acting together and trying anything you want.[9]

Lipinski was not an instant gold medalist on the tour. She discovered there is a lot to learn before you can master a role in such a show. For one thing, she was not always in the spotlight and sometimes had to be a supporting player. She also had to adjust to performing with other people on the ice.

During the first week of rehearsals in Simsbury, Connecticut, for the 1998–1999 tour, she became eager to get on the ice more often. But Bezic and Miller were working on routines involving other skaters, including Ilia Kulik, the men's gold medalist at Nagano, who had joined the tour at the same time as Lipinski.

"You see her watching them rehearse and you can just tell how badly she wants to be out there, too," said her mother. "She can't hold back all that energy and wanting to be involved in everything. It's something new for Tara."[10]

Kristi Yamaguchi, the 1992 Olympic champion

**FACT**

There are certain things Tara Lipinski will not wear. Her skating costumes cannot include anything orange. She does not want sleeveless dresses, puffy sleeves, or sleeves that dangle, and will wear only a few sparkles, beads, or sequins.

who also turned pro soon after her victory in Albertville, France, said Lipinski's passion for skating inspired the veterans of the tour. "For Tara, this is a whole new world," said Yamaguchi.

> I went through something similar. And it's important to this tour, because of the youthful exuberance and young blood she brings. That's something that keeps all of us going.[11]

The show revolved around a clever number in which all of the cast members portrayed clowns. Lipinski was the new clown in the group and she had to learn how to be as wild and funny as the rest of the clowns.

One part of the routine included Lipinski and Hamilton standing face-to-face, with Hamilton believing he was looking into a mirror. But he was actually looking right at Lipinski as she mimicked every move he made. It was a hilarious bit of comedy that proved Tara Lipinski could do more than just spins and jump. Said Hamilton:

> It's hard to come up with something different every year. Everybody here feeds off each other's energy, and with a lot of new people in the show, their excitement . . . feeds our energy level. It's more fun, because if you have the same people every year, you can get complacent at times. You're so accustomed to each other.

> With Tara, no one is more suited to this type of show. She's a very smart person with a wonderful head on her shoulders, because she's had a strong upbringing. She has an open mind and a great level of ability. And she can't wait to get on the ice and be a part of everything.[12]

Lipinski was so busy on tour that the first anniversary of her Olympic victory almost slipped by unnoticed—almost.

The closer the calendar crept to February 20, 1999, the more requests she had for interviews.

On the weekend marking the one-year anniversary of the Olympics, many television sports shows replayed her gold-medal-winning performance. Lipinski had often watched the tapes of the Olympic competition, and each time she understood even more how special those moments were.

"The Olympics changed my whole life," she said.

> At the moment I won, it was, 'It's yours forever. You don't have to give it up.' When I look at the medal, it's so awesome. It may not be as great as it was if I went [to the Olympics] the next time. I'm going on with my life. My plan always was to try to win the Olympics, and I got that a little faster than I thought. Now, it's on to other things, and I don't regret any decisions. I know I've done the right things for my life.[13]

# Chapter 7

# In the Celebrity Spotlight

ara Lipinski is everywhere. Turn on the television set and you are likely to see the 1998 Olympic gold medalist acting in a soap opera or a prime time television show. She gets more time on the air for her commercials than for her skating.

Not that Lipinski is forgetting her roots. She still remains as a headliner for Stars on Ice and occasionally appears in professional competitions.

But she is also branching out, which can mean representing DKNY (a fashion design company), Snapple beverages, DeBeers Company (which processes diamonds), or ESPN's sports magazine. It can mean hosting her own television special, or even writing instructional books.

She earned close to $10 million in everything

from endorsements to books—all before turning seventeen.

"I need new challenges," Lipinski said. "I could be twenty-four or whatever, but I still would have accomplished all I set out to do at sixteen."[1]

So Lipinski took up acting, including a three-month role as Marnie on the soap opera *The Young and the Restless*. She seemed very natural before the camera portraying someone else—no surprise there, considering how often figure skaters are on television, and how they play characters in their skating programs.

Her first TV special, *From the Moment*, received good reviews, and she made appearances on *Touched by an Angel, Veronica's Closet, Candid Camera, Afraid of the Dark*, and *Figure It Out—Wild Style*.

Then there was the television movie comedy *Ice Angel*. Lipinski co-starred in the story of a star hockey player who is accidentally killed. He comes back to life in the body of a seventeen-year-old female figure skater who has been in a coma.

Lipinski played a former competitor of the girl in the coma. She helps the girl recovering from the coma get back into shape—unaware that a boy is in the girl's body.

A whole new area of entertainment was opening

up for her. Would that mean she might abandon the ice pretty soon?

"I love skating, and I could never give it up," Lipinski said. "But doing things like this on the side is fun."[2]

Perhaps to show her devotion to skating, Lipinski still conducts clinics for young skaters. That's something she plans on continuing "forever," she said.

During one clinic in Troy, Michigan, not far from the Detroit Skating Club where she trained for the Olympics, Lipinski gave tips to about three hundred young skaters. She explained how to lift off for jumps, how to spin, how to get in good shape, and how to stay calm and focused for a full program.

It was a typical session for Lipinski, who truly seems to enjoy being with her fans—a trait common to figure skaters.

"There are tons of kids [here]," she said. "Without them, I wouldn't be able to do what I love. For them to be able to meet me makes me feel happy that they're happy about it."[3]

Another thing that has made Lipinski happy is her decision to continue with Stars on Ice. Each season, her role in the show has expanded as she has become more comfortable with being a star entertainer rather than an athlete.

*Tara Lipinski stands at attention during the playing of the national anthem at the Olympics. She has carried the memory of that spectacular moment with her as she brings her devotion to skating to other young skaters.*

That does not mean she is out of shape. And, she has had to deal with the changes in her body as she has matured. Sandra Bezic, who puts together the routines for Stars on Ice, has given Lipinski a more mature look and had her skate to more adult music.

"I have a blast. I look forward the most to touring because it's a high every night. It's like when you are competing, the same rush you get without the nerves," Lipinski said.

"The skating always should be fun, or you shouldn't be doing it. Skating has brought me everything I have, so I never really think of it as work."[4]

But she worked hard enough at fitting in with Stars on Ice that now she is one of the gang—a very impressive gang that includes eight Olympic medal winners.

Scott Hamilton, who has seen just about everything in a quarter century as a figure skater, was most impressed by how quickly Lipinski became a part of the Stars on Ice family.

Said Hamilton of Lipinski:

> From where we started at the beginning, she has come a light-year, as far as confidence level and comfort with the group. At first, I think Tara was a little intimidated or a little overwhelmed. . . . Even though she is a champion, she did not have a lot of experience. She had to

**FACT**

Like most Americans, particularly teenage girls, Tara Lipinski was a big fan of the 1999 Women's World Cup soccer team. "That was so cool," she said of their win. "I was one of the girls going crazy. It's great for women's sport. And they all are great role models."

apply herself, not for the skating, but for fitting in as the youngest ever on our tour.

Now she is confident and comfortable and she understands what she was able to bring to the tour, her bubbly enthusiasm and work ethic. Sometimes you look at her and see a thirty-five-year-old woman, and then you see a kid.[5]

That kid still is a super competitor. In December 1999, she skated in the first major competition of her professional career, the World Pro Championships in Washington, D.C.

Naturally, she won.

Lipinski no longer needs to do the incredibly risky triple combinations she did at the Olympics. She is proud that she is still able to do all six kinds of triples she did in Nagano. But, the constraints of touring mean that she must ration them out in her Stars on Ice performances. In Washington, she did three types of triples in the technical program and three other triples in her free skate.

Her artistry was also brilliant as she beat a field of other professionals that included Switzerland's Denise Biellmann, France's Surya Bonaly, 1994 Olympic gold medalist Oksana Baiul and American Tonia Kwiatkowski.

"When I come to compete, I get just as nervous," Lipinski admitted. "I wasn't as nervous as at the

*Lipinski reacts after completing her short program at the Olympics in Nagano in 1998. As a professional skater, Lipinski no longer needs to perform the incredibly risky moves she did at the Olympics.*

Olympics tonight. There's a slight difference. But I do enjoy this. I did the amateur. I had some fun with that, and now I get to experience this."[6]

Tara Lipinski has enjoyed all kinds of special experiences in less than twenty years. Two years and three months after winning the Olympic gold medal, she graduated from high school.

Nowadays, everyone recognizes her.

"You get used to it," she said of being a celebrity. "It's not so bad. You can make it worse if you think a lot about it. When you realize that people want to meet you and know something about you and you put all of it into perspective, it's fairly easy."

"I feel like the same person I've always been, and hopefully I can keep it that way."[7]

## FACT

Tara Lipinski is a nervous flyer and is scared of heights. She once was supposed to fly to Alabama with Todd Eldredge in a private jet for a show. When she saw how small the airplane was, she canceled her trip.

# Chapter Notes

## Chapter 1. Olympic Wondergirl

1. Author interview of Tara Lipinski, February 21, 1998, Nagano, Japan.

2. Ibid.

3. Ibid.

4. Author interview of Tara Lipinski, February 5, 1998, Nagano, Japan.

5. Author interview of Tara Lipinski, February 17, 1998, Nagano, Japan.

6. Steve Wilstein, "Inside the Rings: Tara and Todd," The Associated Press electronic wire service, February 17, 1998, Nagano, Japan.

7. Ibid.

8. Author interview of Tara Lipinski, February 7, 1998, Nagano, Japan.

9. Ibid.

10. Author interview of Tara Lipinski, February 17, 1998, Nagano, Japan.

11. Author interview of Tara Lipinski, February 18, 1998, Nagano, Japan.

12. Ibid.

13. Ibid.

14. Author interview of Tara Lipinski, February 20, 1998, Nagano, Japan.

15. Ibid.

## Chapter 2. Starting Out

1. Author interview of Pat Lipinski, October 17, 1999, Simsbury, Conn.

2. Ibid.

3. Author interview of Pat and Jack Lipinski, October 17, 1999, Simsbury, Conn.

4. Author interview of Pat Lipinski, October 17, 1999, Simsbury, Conn.

5. Ibid.

6. B.J. Reyes, "Team Tara," The Associated Press electronic wire story, October 14, 1997, Bloomfield Hills, Mich.

7. Author interview of Tara Lipinski, October 17, 1999, Simsbury, Conn..

8. Reyes, "Team Tara," October 14, 1997.

## Chapter 3. The Rivalry Begins

1. Author interview of Kathy Casey, February 7, 1995, Providence, R.I.

2. Ibid.

3. Ibid.

4. Author interview of Michelle Kwan, February 10, 1995, Providence, R.I.

5. Author interview of Michelle Kwan, February 11, 1995, Providence, R.I.

6. Author interview of Tara Lipinski, February 9, 1995, Providence, R.I.

7. Ibid.

8. Author interview of Frank Carroll, October 31, 1999, Colorado Springs, Colo.

9. Author interview of Richard Callaghan, October 31, 1999, Colorado Springs, Colo.

10. Author interview of Todd Eldridge, February 14, 1998, Nagano, Japan.

11. Author interview of Richard Callaghan, January 22, 1996, San Jose, Calif.

12. Ibid.

13. Author interview of Tara Lipinski, March 18, 1996, Edmonton, Alberta, Canada.

14. Ibid.

15. Author interview of Tara Lipinski, March 23, 1996, Edmonton, Alberta, Canada.

## Chapter 4. American Champ, World Champ

1. Author interview of Tara Lipinski, March 1, 1997, Hamilton, Ontario, Canada.

2. Author interview of Sandra Bezic, March 1, 1997, Hamilton, Ontario, Canada.

3. Author interview of Richard Callaghan, October 23, 1997, Detroit, Mich.

4. Author interview of Tara Lipinski, February 14, 1997, Nashville, Tenn.

5. Nancy Armour, "U.S. Skating—Women," The Associated Press electronic wire story, February 15, 1997, Nashville, Tenn.

6. Ibid.

7. Author interview of Tara Lipinski, March 3, 1997, Hamilton, Ontario, Canada.

8. Author interview of Richard Callaghan, March 3, 1997, Hamilton, Ontario, Canada.

9. Colleen Barry, "World Skating," The Associated Press electronic wire story, March 21, 1997, Lausanne, Switzerland.

10. Ibid.

11. Salvatore Zanca, "World Skating," The Associated Press electronic wire story, March 22, 1997, Lausanne, Switzerland.

## Chapter 5. The Olympic Buildup

1. Author interview of Tara Lipinski, October 23, 1997, Detroit, Mich.

2. Author interview of Richard Callaghan, October 23, 1997, Detroit, Mich.

3. Author interview of Tara Lipinski, October 23, 1997, Detroit, Mich.

4. Author interview of Tara Lipinski, October 27, 1997, Detroit, Michigan.

5. Salvatore Zanca, "Lalique Skating," The Associated Press electronic wire story, November 15, 1997, Paris, France.

6. Samantha Perry, "Exchange—Figure Skater," The Associated Press electronic wire story, November 24, 1997, Bluefield, W. Va.

7. Nancy Armour, "USOC Sportswoman," The Associated Press electronic wire story, December 17, 1997.

8. Colleen Barry, "Skating Champions," The Associated Press electronic wire story, December 18, 1997, Munich, Germany.

9. Nancy Armour, "Going for Gold," The Associated Press electronic wire story, January 3, 1998.

10. Nancy Armour, "U.S. Skating—Women," The Associated Press electronic wire story, January 8, 1998, Philadelphia, Penn.

11. Nancy Armour, "U.S. Skating—Women," The Associated Press electronic wire story, January 9, 1998, Philadelphia, Penn.

12. Author interview of Tara Lipinski, January 9, 1998, Philadelphia, Penn.

13. Author interview of Frank Carroll, January 9, 1998, Philadelphia, Penn.

## Chapter 6. The Big Decision

1. Author interview of Tara Lipinski, February 20, 1998, Nagano, Japan.

2. Ibid., April 8, 1998, New York.

3. Joseph White, "Olympians Dispute," The Associated Press electronic wire story, April 29, 1998, Washington, D.C.

4. Ibid.

5. Author interview of Tara Lipinski, February 16, 1999, New York.

6. Author interview of Tara Lipinski, May 11, 1998, New York.

7. Author interview of Kurt Ascherman, May 11, 1998, New York.

8. Author interview of Tara Lipinski, May 11, 1998, New York.

9. Author interview of Tara Lipinski, August 20, 1998, New York.

10. Author interview of Pat Lipinski October 6, 1998, Simsbury, Conn.

11. Author interview of Kristi Yamaguchi, October 6, 1998, Simsbury, Conn.

12. Author interview of Scott Hamilton, October 6, 1998, Simsbury, Conn.

13. Author interview of Tara Lipinski, October 6, 1998, Simsbury, Conn.

## Chapter 7. In the Celebrity Spotlight

1. Salvatore Zanca, "Faded Glory," The Associated Press electronic wire story, March 20, 1999, Helsinki, Finland.

2. Author interview of Tara Lipinski, May 30, 1999, New York.

3. "Names in the Game," The Associated Press electronic wire story, May 31, 1999.

4. Author interview of Tara Lipinski, October 17, 1999, Simsbury, Conn.

5. Author interview of Scott Hamilton, October 17, 1999, Simsbury, Conn.

6. Joseph White, "World Pro Skating," The Associated Press electronic wire story, December 11, 1999, Washington, D.C.

7. Author interview of Tara Lipinski, March 1, 2000, New York.

# Glossary

**compulsory figures**—The tracing of figure eights on the ice. These figures are no longer done in competition.

**double axel**—A difficult jump in competition that requires an extra half turn in the air. It is a two-and-a-half revolution jump. The axel is the only jump that begins from the forward outside edge of the skate. It is landed on the back outside edge of the opposite foot.

**figure eight**—A skating pattern in which a performer's motions form the shape of the number eight on the ice.

**free skate**—The second portion of competition for solo and pairs skaters. It is worth two thirds of the skater's total score, and skaters may perform anything they choose—within the rules of figure skating.

**intermediate level**—The easiest level of skating for a serious figure skater. This level is followed by the novice level.

**International Skating Union (ISU)**—The governing body for international figure skating and speed skating.

**junior level**—The level of skating for serious figure skaters that follows novice level.

**long program**—*See also*, free skate.

**Lutz**—A figure skating move in which a skater jumps from the outer edge of one foot, does one, two, or three rotations while in the air, and lands on the other foot.

**National Championships**—The event in which the top novice, junior, and senior level skaters compete for United States titles.

**novice level**—The level of skating for serious figure skaters that follows intermediate level.

**pairs**—A team of skaters composed of one male and one female. The team performs together in competitions. Pairs skating differs from ice dancing in that in pairs, skaters are permitted to do lifts above the shoulder, throws, and jumps.

**quadruple jump**—Any jump requiring four turns in the air.

**regionals**—The first level of competition on the way to nationals.

**sectionals**—The level that follows regionals. Medal winners in sectionals automatically go to the national championships.

**senior level**—The highest level of skating for serious figure skaters.

**stroke**—The method that skaters use to progress across the ice. Even advanced skaters like Michelle Kwan take stroking classes to build power and speed.

**technical program**—The first of two programs skated by solo and pairs skaters. It is worth one third of the total score. There are eight required moves in a technical program.

**triple Salchow**—A jump in which the skater takes off from the back inside edge of one foot and lands backward on the outside edge of the opposite foot. The skater performs three turns in the air.

**United States Championships**—The highest prize in Olympic-eligible competitions in American figure skating.

**United States Olympic Committee (USOC)**—The governing body for Olympic sports in the United States.

**World Championships**—An important annual competition in figure skating where top Olympic-level skaters from around the world compete.

**World Professional Championships**—An important annual competition for professional skaters who are no longer eligible for the Olympics.

# Career Statistics

## Competitive Highlights

| | | |
|---|---|---|
| 1999 | World Pro Championships | 1st |
| 1998 | Olympic Games | 1st |
| 1998 | U.S. Championships | 2nd |
| 1998 | Champions Series Final | 1st |
| 1997 | World Championships | 1st |
| 1997 | Champions Series Final | 1st |
| 1997 | U.S. Championships | 1st |
| 1997 | Skate America | 2nd |
| 1996 | Nations Cup | 2nd |
| 1996 | Trophee Lalique | 3rd |
| 1996 | Skate Canada | 2nd |
| 1996 | World Championships | 15th |
| 1996 | U.S. Championships | 3rd |
| 1996 | World Junior Championships* | 5th |
| 1995 | U.S. Championships (Junior) | 2nd |
| 1995 | World Junior Championships* | 4th |
| 1994 | U.S. Olympic Festival | 1st |
| 1994 | U.S. Championships (Novice) | 2nd |

*These competitions actually took place in November of the previous year.

# Where to Write Tara Lipinski

Ms. Tara Lipinski
c/o Edge Marketing
1808 E. Boulevard
Charlotte, NC 28203

## Internet Addresses

*Tara Lipinski's Official Web site*
<http://www.taralipinski.com>

*United States Figure Skating Association (USFSA)*
<http://www.usfsa.org>

*International Skating Union (ISU)*
<http://www.isu.org>

# Index